A
SHORT
HISTORY

Editor: Meredith Wolf Schizer
Designer: T. R. Nimen
Production Manager: Elizabeth Gaynor

Original concept and research by Joan Slomanson

First edition
2 4 6 8 10 9 7 5 3 1

Library of Congress Cataloging-in-Publication Data
Slomanson, Joan Kanel.
A short history: thumbnail sketches of 50 little giants / by Joan Kanel
Slomanson ; illustrated by T. R. Nimen.
p. cm.
ISBN 0-7892-0333-2
1. Short people—Biography. 2. Celebrities—Biography.
I. Title.
CT105.S63 1998
920.02—dc21   97-9911

Grateful acknowledgment is made to DDB Needham for permission
to use the Volkswagen "Think Small" ad, and to the *New York Times*
for permission to reprint an excerpt from an interview with Fran
Lebowitz in James Atlas's article, "What They Look Like to the Rest
of Us," November 19, 1995. Copyright © 1995 by The New York
Times Co. Reprinted by permission.

A SHORT HISTORY

Thumbnail Sketches of 50 Little Giants

Joan Kanel Slomanson

Illustrated by T. R. Nimen

Abbeville Press Publishers

New York   London   Paris

It is good for me that I am not a tall man. Why? Because I must be quick! quick! and a tall man is always slow. It is so through all professions. The best men are not too high. All the mean, cunning men that I have known—short! All the keen, eager, ambitious men—short! And for work—the tall man has too much to carry, he is too far from the ground, he cannot lose and recover balance as is necessary—in a flash.

—*Harry Houdini*

The person who makes money is invariably short. Very short. . .The majority of billion-aires in this country are below-average height. I once found myself standing in the midst of a number of these men, and it looked like the wrap party from The Wizard of Oz.

—*Fran Lebowitz*

To my mother and father, Lee and Jack Kanel,
who made me what I am today:
short.

Table of Contents

Introduction

A tall friend of mine brags that her baby is "well over the average in length." To show pride or confidence, one is advised to "stand tall" or "walk tall." And I once heard a physician say that his hospital's doctors were obviously better than those at a rival institution because most of them were six-footers.

The idea for this little book came to me after a flight in which an entire pro basketball team shared my section of the plane. Thanks to their gargantuan size, these young men didn't so much occupy the plane as own it. Yet aside from the fact that their height enables them to slam-dunk a ball into a basket, they might be otherwise inferior to any shorter person. Be that as it may, most of the world tends to lend greater importance to height.

It's time to change this misguided mind-set and pay homage to some of the many individuals who have made a name for themselves in spite of—and sometimes because of—their short stature. The men included here are all five feet four or under, and the women are five feet one or under.

In truth, my list of short people who made it big grew so long, some people whom you may have expected to see here will have to wait for a second volume to make an appearance. Or perhaps those people are not or were not as gloriously short as you thought them to be.

JKS

GRACIE ALLEN

1906–1964

For decades, the comedy team of Burns and
Allen kept America in stitches, with Gracie
Allen's wacky persona making the perfect foil
to her straight-man husband, George Burns.*
According to Burns, little Gracie once insisted
that six inches be cut off the backseat of
their limo so her feet could touch the floor.
As a result, nobody else could sit there
without falling off.

Under 5′

*With age Burns became extremely short, but in the old days he was
much taller than Allen.

CLARA BARTON

1821–1912

Her size and sex notwithstanding, Barton
wanted to be a Union soldier. When that
proved impossible, this delicate-looking
woman became the Civil War's Angel of the
Battlefield, nursing, comforting, and bringing
supplies to the wounded under horrendous
conditions. Inspired by this experience, she
went on to become the founder, in 1881,
of the American Red Cross.

5′

LUDWIG VAN BEETHOVEN

1770–1827

Although Beethoven and Napoleon Bonaparte
were the same height, they didn't see eye
to eye. Beethoven ripped Bonaparte's name
off a symphony written in honor of France's
ruler when Napoleon proclaimed himself
emperor in May 1804. Still composing when
he could no longer hear, Beethoven "listened"
to his string quartets by following the
motion of the bows.

5'4"

DAVID BEN-GURION

1886–1973

David Green, born in Poland, took the name
of an ancient freedom fighter, Ben-Gurion.
The modern-day Ben-Gurion had been a
scrawny little child, yet even then he was
said to be head and shoulders above his
peers. Elected as Israel's first prime minister
and minister of defense after the War of
Independence, "the Old Man" is revered as
the Father of the Nation.

About 5′

TYRONE (MUGGSY) BOGUES

b. 1965

The shortest player in the history of the
National Basketball Association, this
minuscule point guard has made a record
number of assists for the Charlotte Hornets.
A phenomenon among the NBA giants,
Bogues uses speed, guile, guts, and
enthusiasm to make up for lack of height.
"He's always around you like a mosquito,"
said an admiring opponent. Or like a hornet?

5′3″

NAPOLEON BONAPARTE

1769–1821

The humble Little Corporal who made himself
the high-and-mighty emperor of France,
Napoleon I fought his way to glory on the
battlefields of Europe. Le Petit Tendu
("the little crop-head"), as he was called in
his youth, finally met his Waterloo in June
1815 and went into exile. Today, his name is
mainly associated with the civil code of
France and a cream-filled pastry.

5′4″

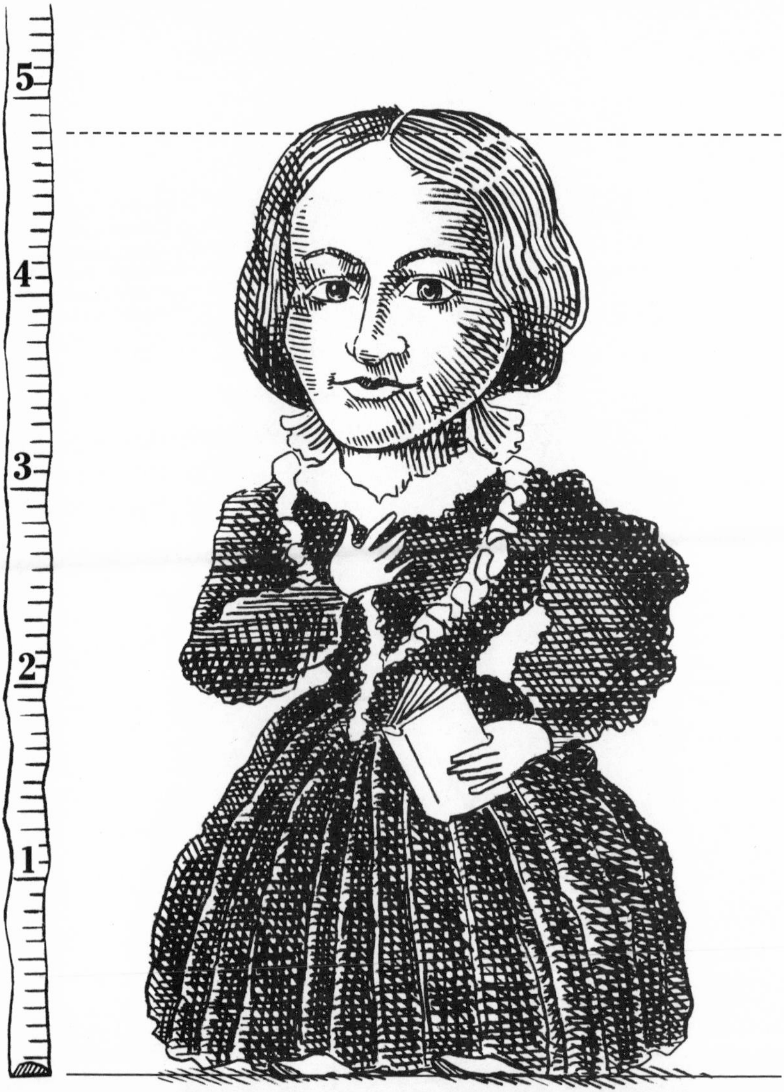
5
4
3
2
1

CHARLOTTE BRONTË

1816–1855

The novelist William Makepeace Thackeray called her "a little bit of a creature without a penny worth of good looks." So tiny her garments looked like doll's clothes, this smallest* Brontë built a vast fantasy world in stories and pictures with her sisters and brother. Using fingers she herself described as bird's claws, Brontë wrote her way to fame with such enduring classics as *Jane Eyre* (1847).

4'10"

*Emily Brontë was a towering five foot six. Brother Branwell was only five foot three.

TRUMAN CAPOTE

1924–1984

Described as looking like a small child when he was a copyboy at the *New Yorker*, Capote was later called the Little God by publications fighting over his short stories. In the years that followed, works such as *Breakfast at Tiffany's* (1958) and *In Cold Blood* (1966) brought him fame, while the outrageous way he wrote about his society friends made him somewhat infamous.

5'3"

ANDREW CARNEGIE

1835–1919

"The tiny personification of the Age of
Steel,"* this immigrant from an impoverished
family built a gigantic industrial empire.
But he is best remembered for his
philanthropy. Once the richest man in the
world, Carnegie gave away over 90 percent
of his fortune to create foundations,
endowments, educational facilities,
and 3,000 libraries around the globe.

Just over 5′

*As described by David Levering Lewis, in *W.E.B. Du Bois: Biography
of a Race 1868–1919* (1993).

27

NANCY CURRIE

b. 1958

Aboard the U.S. space shuttle *Discovery*
in 1995, the world's littlest space traveler
discovered what it's like to be taller.
This tiny astronaut, an army major and
mission specialist, *grew* an inch or two after
arriving in orbit. Apparently, the absence
of gravity allows the spine to stretch.
But Currie was destined to revert to her
original height upon landing.

5' (when on earth)

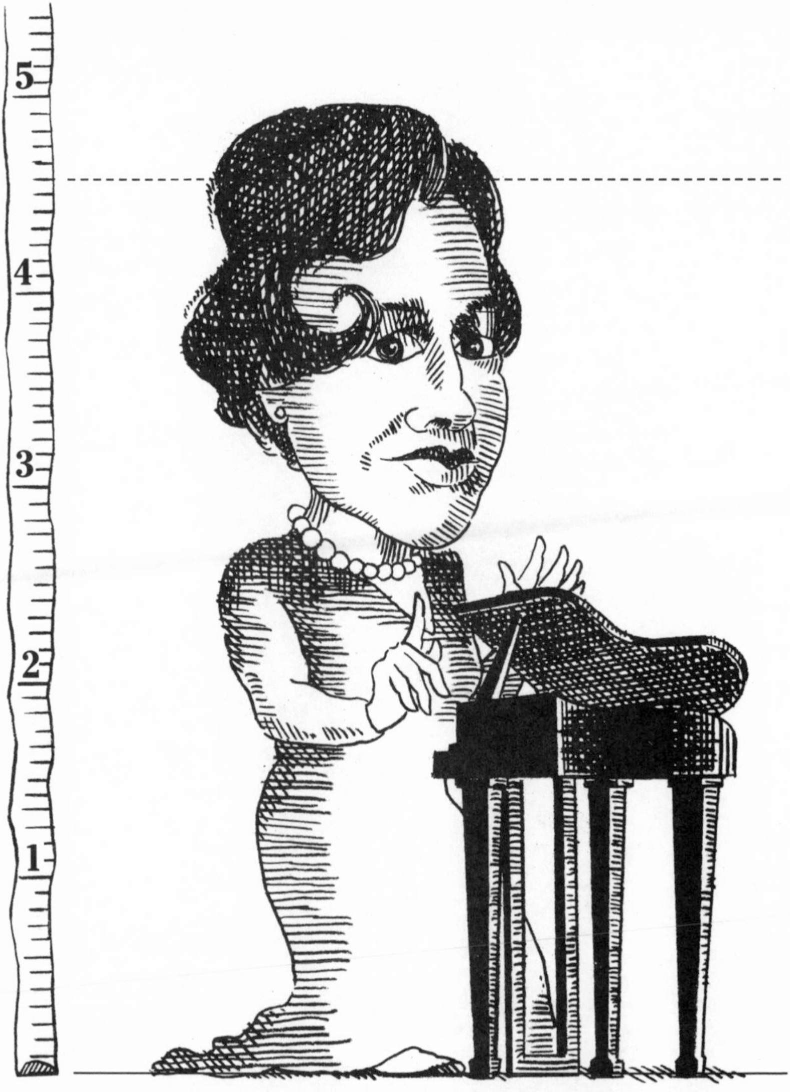
5
4
3
2
1

ALICIA DE LARROCHA

b. 1923

Although she has shrunk from four foot nine,
this Catalonian virtuoso is every inch a
concert artist. Praised year after year as the
Queen of Pianists, de Larrocha plays a wide-
ranging repertory with astonishing velocity
and clarity, made all the more remarkable by
the fact that her childlike hands have trouble
stretching beyond an octave.

4'5" or 4'6"

THOMAS DE QUINCEY

1785–1859

After writing *Confessions of an English Opium-Eater* (1822), this nineteenth-century addict and essayist was vilified by the press. One paper called him "a five-feet-high animal," looking like one of "those queer big-headed caricatures." But the poets William Wordsworth and Samuel Taylor Coleridge (also an opium addict) admired the intellect of their friend, "little Mr. De Q."

5′

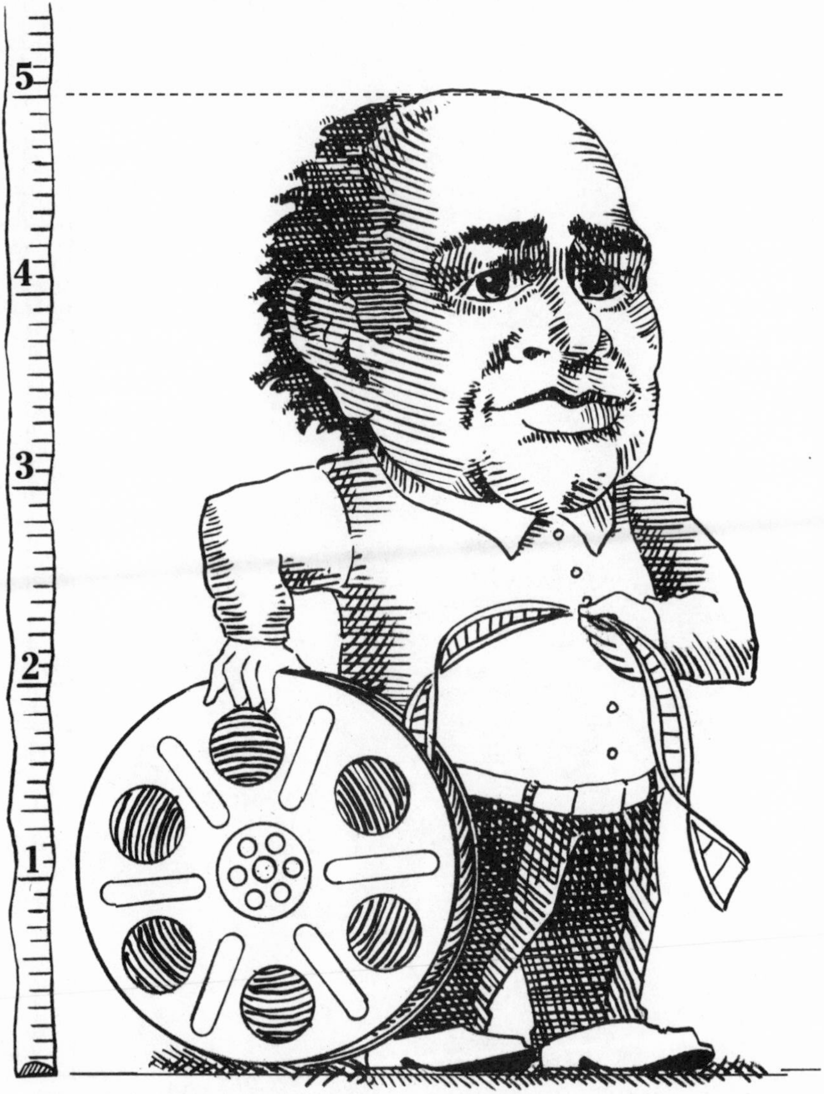
5
4
3
2
1

DANNY DEVITO

b. 1944

The short guy who usually plays
short-tempered characters, Danny DeVito
became a household face as Louie DePalma
in the long-running television series *Taxi*.
In movie after movie, this actor-director-
producer's lack of height seems to
work in his favor. Just watch the way he
upstages any tall, glamorous actress or even
someone like Arnold Schwarzenegger.

5'

ALFRED EISENSTAEDT

1898–1995

Eisie, as everyone called him, was a
Life photographer for fifty-nine years and a
working photographer even longer. A pioneer
in photojournalism, he and his small Leica
were on the job well into his nineties. When a
television interviewer called him "a little big
man with a camera," Eisenstaedt said,
"No, I'm a little *little* man with a camera."

5'4"*

*In the interview mentioned here, Eisenstaedt was said to be barely over
five feet tall, but he himself told this writer that he was five foot four.

EDDY GAEDEL

1925–1961

The shortest major-league baseball player on record, Gaedel pinch-hit for the Saint Louis Browns in 1951 wearing the number "1/8" on his uniform. In his one at-bat, this tiny terror walked on four pitches thanks to his microscopic one-and-one-half-inch strike zone. Small wonder that right after Gaedel's feat, height restrictions were written into the rules effective the following year.

3'7"

LORENZ HART

1895–1943

Larry Hart was the lyricist who wrote a thousand songs and countless Broadway shows with composer Richard Rodgers. Described as having the body, hands, and feet of a child, the diminutive Hart was nonetheless looked up to by show business cronies like Alan Jay Lerner* and Joshua Logan, the director who called Hart a "colossus of talent."

Just under 5'

*Lerner estimated Hart's height at about four foot ten, which may be closer to the truth, since Hart called the lifts in his shoes "two-inch liars."

HELEN HAYES

1900–1993

At eighteen, Helen Hayes was already called
"the teeniest big star on the stage." And in
1931, the First Lady of the Theater became
the First Lady of the Screen, winning an
Oscar for her role in her very first movie,
The Sin of Madeline Claudet.* But a real test
of her talent came when Broadway's shortest
leading lady portrayed history's tallest
queen in *Mary of Scotland* (1933).

5′

*Another first: Hayes was the first woman to be elected a member of
New York's esteemed theatrical club, The Players.

JOSEPH HIRSHHORN

1899–1981

Best known for the Washington, D.C., museum bearing his name, the Joseph H. Hirshhorn Museum and Sculpture Garden, Hirshhorn was the self-made multimillionaire who donated one of the world's largest personal art collections to the United States. Described as "*famously* small . . . [with] an outsize personality,"* he enjoyed telling the story about when "tiny little Joe Hirshhorn" visited "great big Lyndon Johnson" in the White House.

5′4″

*According to art critic John Russell.

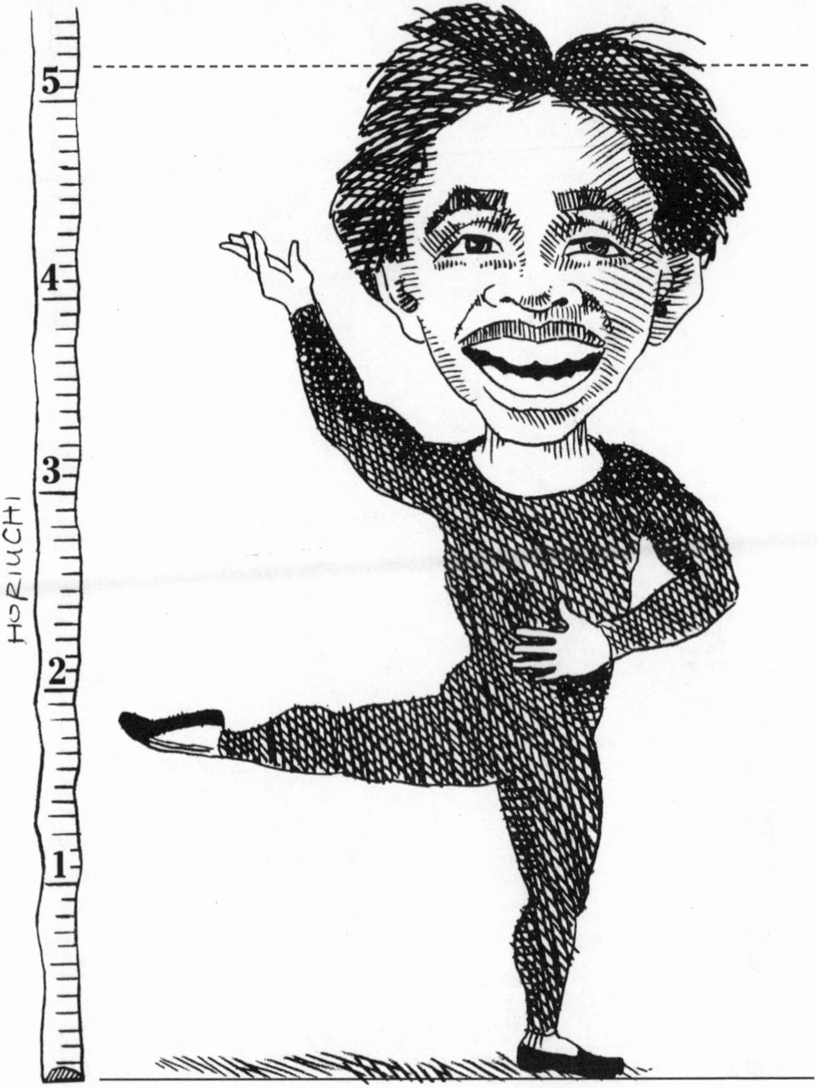
5
4
3
2
1
HORIUCHI

GEN HORIUCHI

b. 1965

From the ballet stage to Broadway, this
little Japanese-born dancer has astonished
audiences with his vigor and virtuosity.
While he has rarely tried to lift tall ballerinas,
his multiple, miniature turns and jumps
are perfectly and fearlessly executed.
And when he comes back to earth,
the smile of satisfaction on his face makes
his fans go wild.

5'2"

HARRY HOUDINI

1874–1926

The Great Houdini, master magician and
"death-defying" escape artist, attributed
a variety of heights to himself on passports
and visas. But five foot four is the height he
put on the earliest available adult-age
document—before he started changing his
place of birth from Budapest to Appleton,
Wisconsin, and the color of his eyes
from brown to blue.

Maybe 5'4" (maybe not)

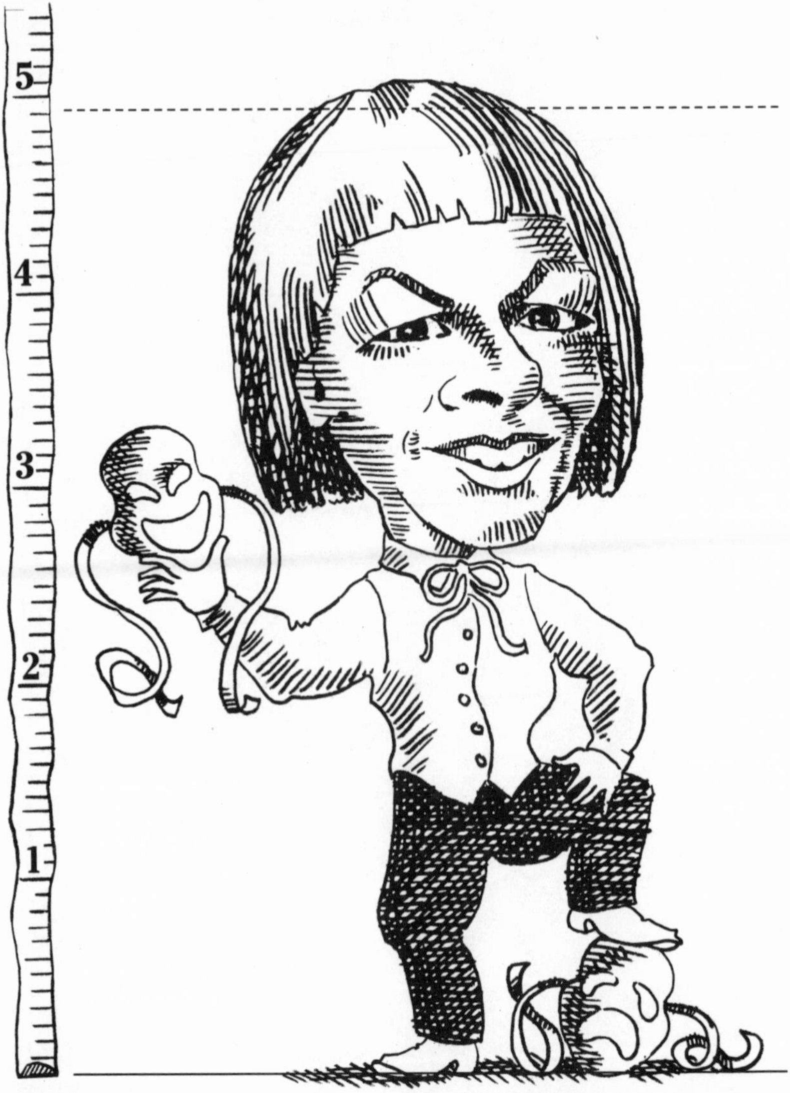
5
4
3
2
1

LINDA HUNT

b. 1945

For her role in *The Year of Living Dangerously*
(1982), Hunt won the first Academy Award
given to anyone acting as a character of the
opposite sex. Her talent is so large, she has
played parts designed for actors a foot taller.
Taking all this success in stride, Hunt told
New Yorker writer Cynthia Zarin, "I live my
life baby step by baby step."

4'9"

KING IBN TALAL HUSSEIN OF JORDAN

b. 1935

Thrust into his present role while still in his teens, Hussein was once dubbed "PLK," short for "Plucky Little King," by journalists who admired the young man's nerve and verve. Through the years, the nickname has proven apt for a leader who often pilots his own jet while standing his ground in the troubled Middle East.

5'3"*

*A reliable source states that he is five foot three, though another source says five foot four.

JOAN OF ARC
1412?–1431

Nobody really knows what the Maid of
Orléans looked like. But a fifteenth-century
suit of armor for a female five-footer was
recently found, and in her day, Saint Joan was
the only woman riding around in men's
clothes. Just imagine France's little heroine
leading the troops while weighted down by a
122-piece, thirty-six-pound steel suit.

Probably 5'

JOHN KEATS

1795–1821

Lord Byron called him a mannikin instead of a
man. Percy Shelley saw him as a symbol of
neglected genius. Yet in his short life (just
twenty-five years), Keats created sonnets that
rank him among the nineteenth century's
greatest poets. "I being stunted am taken for
nothing," he claimed, but as a child he once
fought a big bully who was torturing a
kitten—and won.

5'

FIORELLO LAGUARDIA

1882–1947

Called the Little Flower, a translation of his
first name, this New York City mayor (from
1934 to 1945) won fame for the dramatic ways
in which he fought corruption. To play the
lead in the musical *Fiorello!*, Tom Bosley had
to make himself look smaller. He did so,
according to Marc Kirkeby, by projecting
"the inner fire that can drive short people
to do great things."

5'2"

IRVING (SWIFTY) LAZAR

1907–1993

Nicknamed Swifty by Humphrey Bogart after landing several roles for Bogey in a single day, Lazar was "smaller than a minute, but bigger than life."* King of the Hollywood agents, he was as famed for his Oscar-night parties as for his deals. Yet at one such affair, someone noticed that Lazar, standing, wasn't much taller than Elizabeth Taylor, seated.

5'2"

*Quote is from Annette Tapert, who collaborated with Lazar on his autobiography.

HARRY LIPSIG

1902–1995

This brilliant lawyer, known as the King of Torts, championed the plight of accident victims for six decades. Seeing himself as a modern day David fighting for the "little people" against insurance company goliaths,* Lipsig brought juries to tears. In fact, one jury was so moved by Lipsig's eloquence, they gave the victim *twice* the staggering sum he had asked for.

5'3"

*According to Robert McG. Thomas Jr., writer of Lipsig's *New York Times* obituary.

LILYA LITVYAK

1921–1943

Imagine a fighter pilot so little, she needed
pillows behind her to reach the controls.
Litvyak, the Soviet airwoman called the
Rose of Stalingrad, shot down twelve Nazi
planes, including a balloon that airmen were
afraid to approach. Years later, in 1989, the
aircraft and body of a tiny woman pilot were
found, and Litvyak received her nation's
highest award, posthumously.

Very small and short

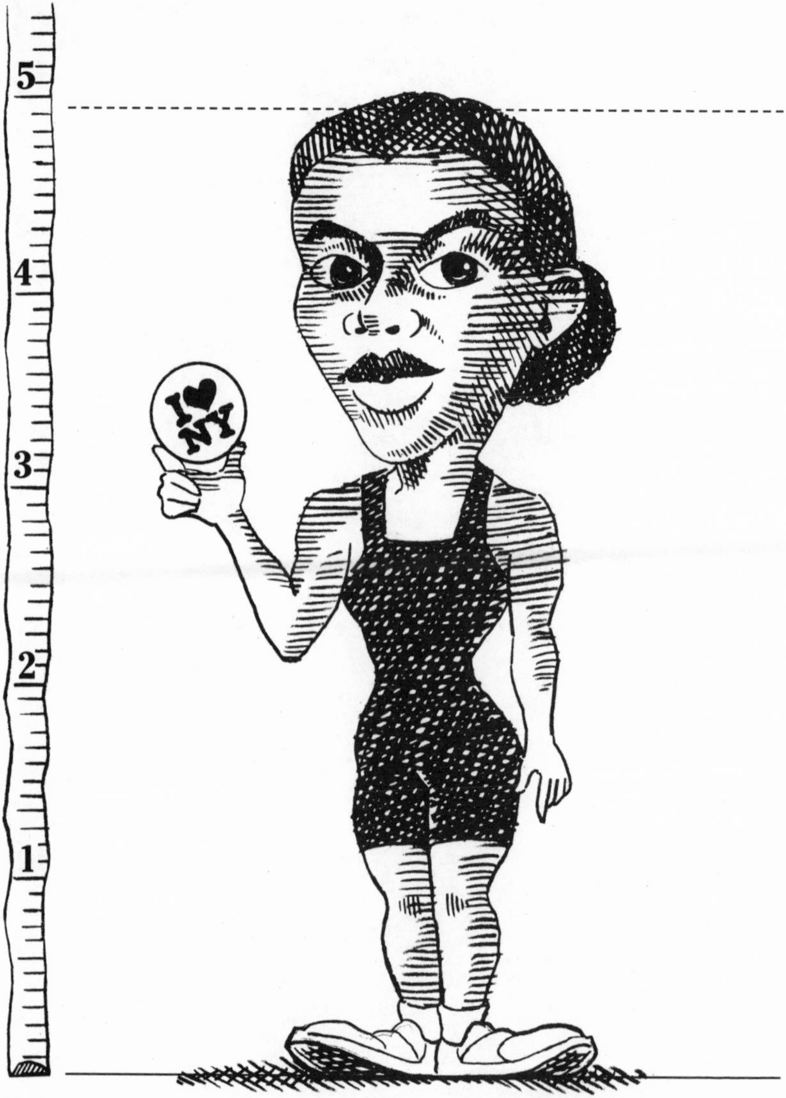
5
4
3
2
1
I ♥ NY

TEGLA LOROUPE

b. 1973

Upon becoming the first black African woman
to win a major marathon, Loroupe received
$20,000, a Mercedes-Benz, and—from her
government—nine head of cattle and sixteen
sheep. Considered extremely swift, especially
for someone so small, she brought pride
to the women of Kenya when she won the
New York City Marathon two years running.

4'11"

JAMES MADISON

1751–1836

His wife called him "the great little Madison,"
but Washington Irving wrote that the fourth
(and shortest) U.S. president (1809–17)
looked like a withered little applejohn,* and
another critic laughed at his "little round hat
and huge cockade." Nonetheless, this
hundred-pound Virginian was elected and
reelected, handily beating not one but two
tall candidates named Clinton.

5'4"

*An old variety of apple, of which the flavor was said to be improved
by drying.

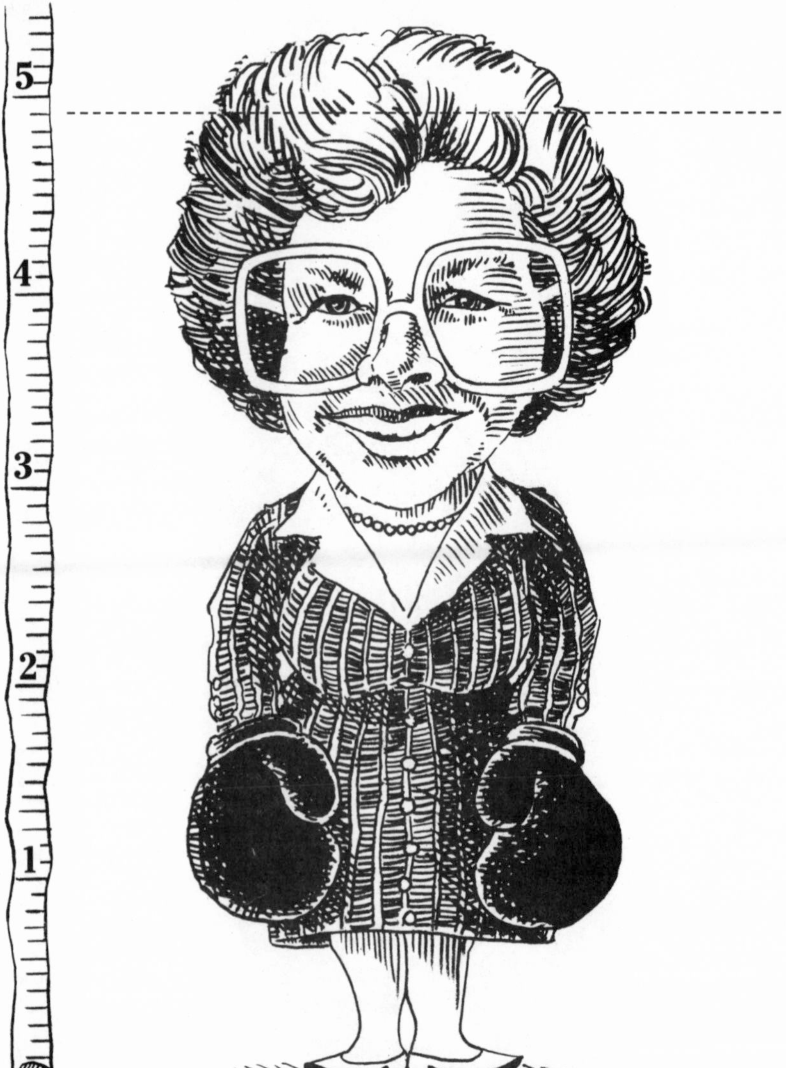
5
4
3
2
1

SENATOR BARBARA MIKULSKI

b. 1936

One of the shortest people in the
U.S. Senate*, this feisty Marylander was
the first Democratic woman to serve in
both houses of Congress. *Time* described her
as a four-foot-eleven bundle of energy with a
voice like a Baltimore Harbor foghorn.
A fighter for women's and working people's
rights, Mikulski uses her voice to blast all
forms of discrimination.

4'11"

*Senator Barbara Boxer is also four foot eleven.

THE HONORABLE ALFRED MOORE

1755–1810

Nominated to the U.S. Supreme Court in 1800 by President John Adams, Justice Moore was described as "so small . . . he seemed only a child." Despite his dwarflike appearance, he had served as a commander in the American Revolution and later became a dominant force at the North Carolina bar, where he was known for his legal brilliance and biting tongue.

4′5″

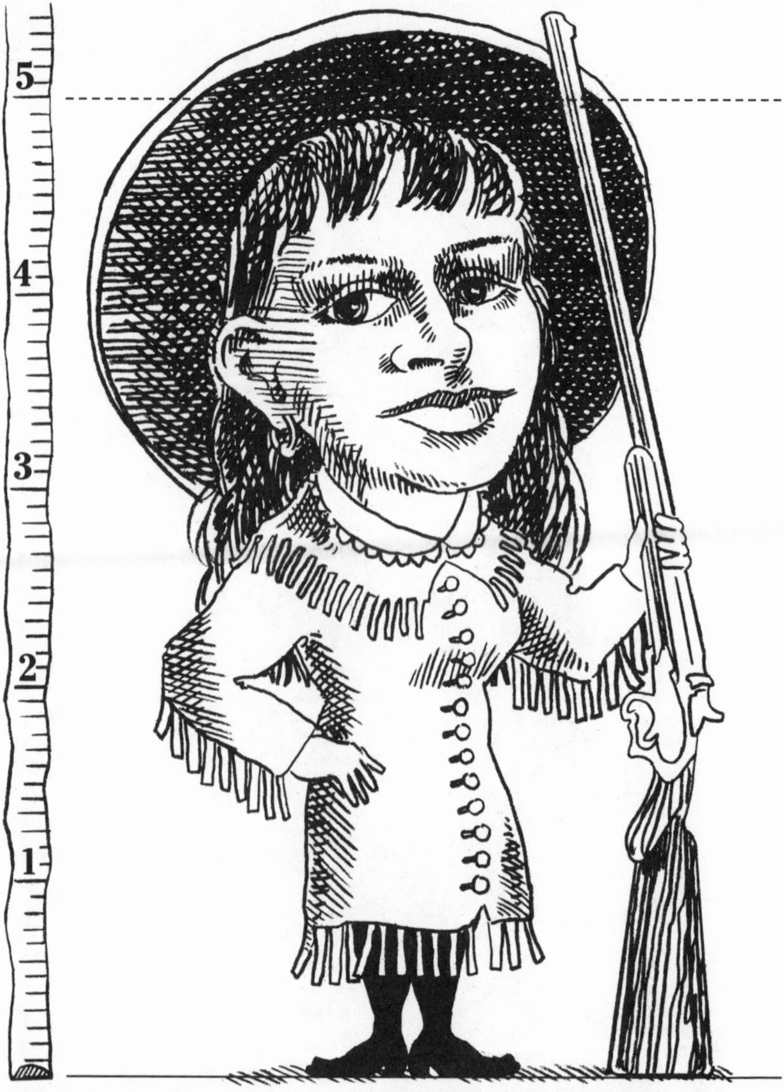
5
4
3
2
1

ANNIE OAKLEY

1860–1926

Immortalized in Irving Berlin's musical
Annie Get Your Gun (1946), Oakley actually
was a traveling performer in Buffalo Bill's
Wild West Show. Her costar and buddy,
Sitting Bull, always spoke of Oakley as
"Little Sure Shot." It's the perfect name for a
short-statured woman who could shoot out
the flames of a revolving wheel of candles
while standing on a galloping horse.

5′

EDITH PIAF

1915–1963

Named Piaf—Parisian slang, meaning
"little sparrow"—by the nightclub owner who
took her under his wing, this celebrated
chanteuse started her career at the age of
fifteen as a lowly street singer. Also called
La Môme ("the kid"), she astonished
audiences with a voice of extraordinary
strength and passion for such a waiflike,
frail-looking woman.

4'8"

LILY PONS

1904–1976

Although she was the daintiest little diva
ever to star at the Metropolitan Opera,
Pons sang some of the most demanding arias.
The Met's leading coloratura soprano for
over twenty-five years, she once appeared
onstage wrapped in cellophane to resemble a
bottle of bubbly. When she burst into song,
listeners said her voice sparkled like . . .
champagne!

5'1"

AUGUSTE RODIN

1840–1917

The great French sculptor of *The Thinker*
(1879–1900) and *The Kiss* (1886) projected
such a powerful image, no one seemed to
notice he was short. Instead, people
invariably mentioned Rodin's enormous
hands and muscular fingers, which could
shape the most delicate works of art.
"To understand these lines," he claimed,
"so tenderly modelled . . . one has to be
lucky enough to be in love."

5′4″

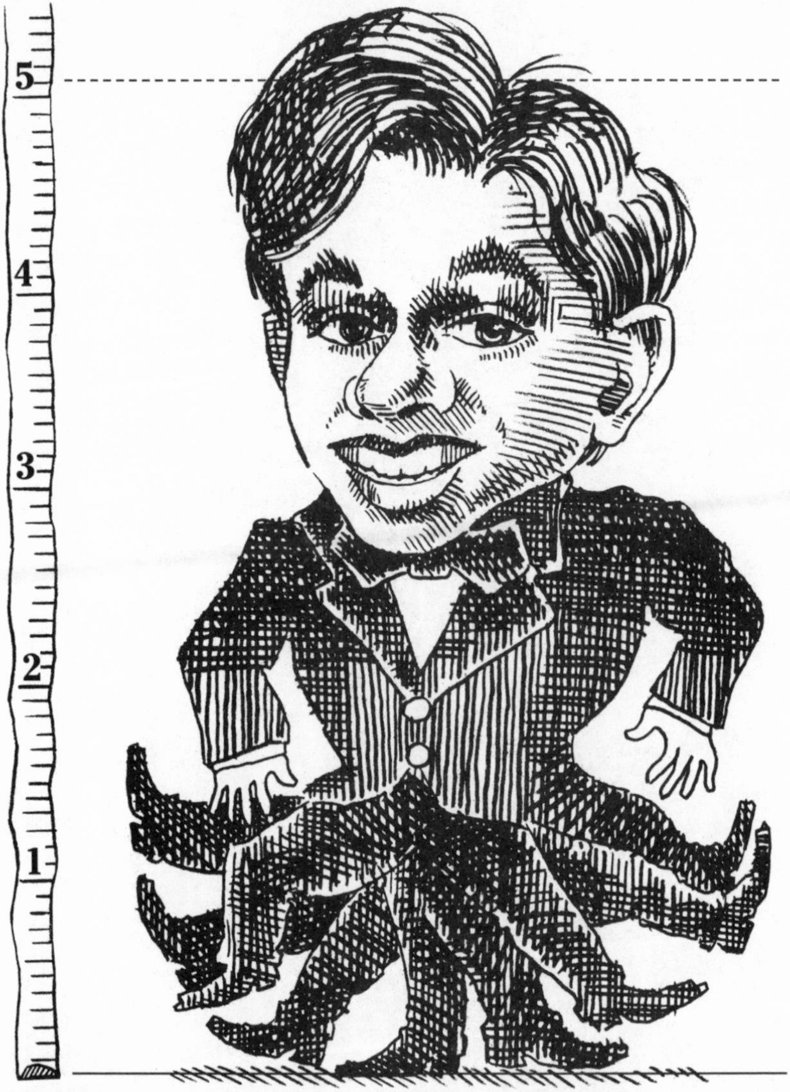
5
4
3
2
1

MICKEY ROONEY

b. 1920

On stage at seventeen months and in the
spotlight ever after, Rooney played kid parts
and jockeys for several decades. "I was a
gnomish prodigy," he says, a "man-child,
child-man." Like most of his eight wives,
Ava Gardner seemed to tower over Rooney,
yet he claims that she was as short as he is,
fooling the public by wearing very
high platform heels.

5'1"

JOHNNY ROVENTINI
b. 1913

This teeny-weeny bellhop, discovered while
paging in a hotel, rose to fame yelling out the
advertising slogan, "Call for Philip Morris."
Once referred to as the world's richest
callboy, he seems an odd choice to represent
a tobacco company, since parents used to
warn their children that cigarettes would
stunt their growth.

3′11″

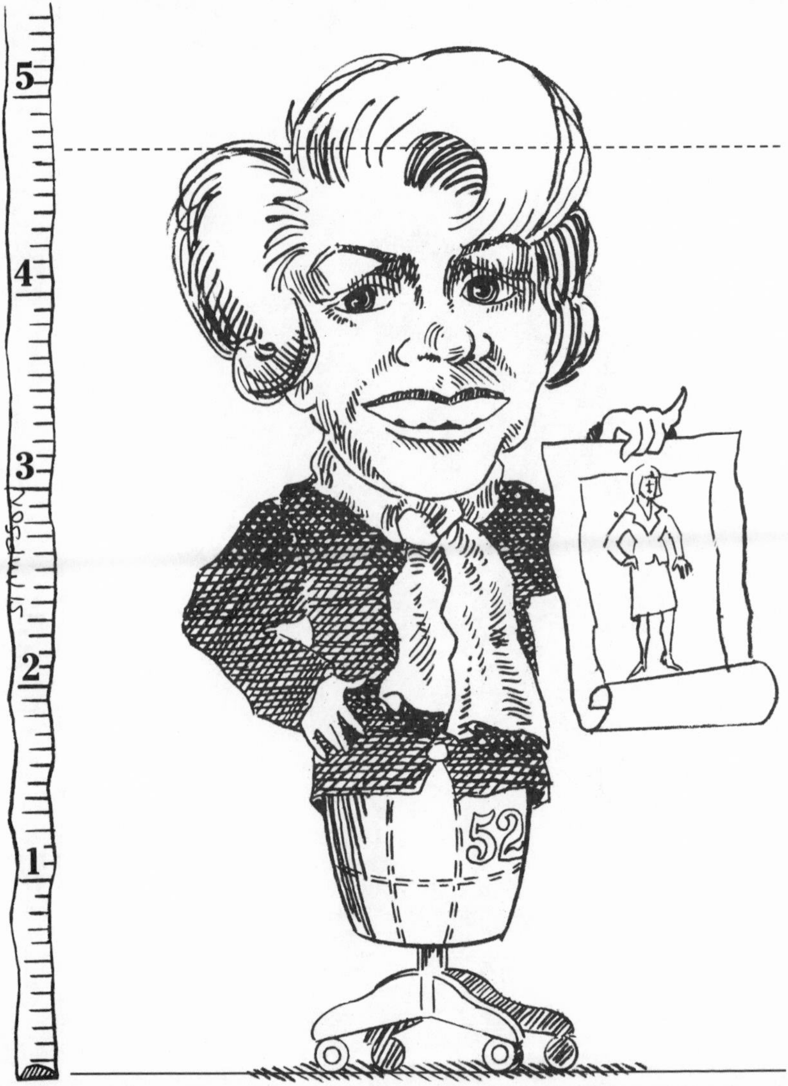
5
4
3
2
1
52

ADELE SIMPSON

1903–1995

In her advertising, this famous couturier
was shown standing on a ladder to reach and
fit models who towered over her. Despite her
own size, Simpson knew how to flatter all
figures—to such an extent that her sales
figures were often the highest in her field, and
her becoming styles were popular with a
succession of America's First Ladies.

4'9"

CHARLES PROTEUS STEINMETZ

1865–1923

Heralded as a modern Jupiter, the German-born Steinmetz was one of the world's greatest electrical engineers and General Electric's best-known scientist. A tiny hunchback, he was given the nickname "Proteus" by his classmates at the University of Breslau in Germany because they felt he resembled the minuscule Greek god, who was said to possess all the knowledge in the world.

Barely 4′

HARRIET BEECHER STOWE

1811–1896

By her own self-deprecating description, the author of *Uncle Tom's Cabin* (1852) was "a little bit of a woman . . . as thin and dry as a pinch of snuff . . . looking like a used-up article." But President Abraham Lincoln saw more vitality in Stowe. On meeting her he exclaimed, "So you're the little woman who wrote the book that started this great war!'"

4'11"*

*Definitely under five feet tall, Stowe may have been even shorter than four foot eleven.

IGOR STRAVINSKY

1882–1971

Taunted at school because of his short
stature, Stravinsky grew to be one of the
greatest modern composers. In fact, his
Le Sacre du Printemps (*The Rite of Spring*,
1913) was once called "the most important
symphonic creation of the twentieth
century." When he conducted an orchestra,
he was so energetically alive, he was
said to resemble a small bird with quick,
electric movements.

5'4"

NAIM SULEYMANOGLU

b. 1967

In 1996 the man called Pocket Hercules
became the first Olympic weight lifter to win
three gold medals. The only known mortal
who can lift three times his body weight, this
undersized powerhouse began setting world
records in Bulgaria. Defecting to Turkey, he
won not only medals, but freedom for many
of his compatriots, the adoration of millions,
and enormous wealth.

4'11"

MOTHER TERESA

1910–1997

Born Agnes Bojaxhiu, this diminutive winner
of the 1979 Nobel Peace Prize has been
called the world's strongest woman. She
found her true calling in the slums of
Calcutta, founding the Missionaries of Charity
there in 1948 to minister to the sick and
dying. Today, her group's arduous work is
worldwide, but she has said, "I am nothing
but a pencil in God's hands."

4'11"

HENRI DE TOULOUSE-LAUTREC

1864–1901

Although he suffered from a form of dwarfism that made walking painful, Lautrec acquired the self-discipline to develop his artistic talent. Born to an aristocratic family, he found inspiration in the Parisian underworld. "Ugliness," he said, "always has a beautiful side," which could explain the appeal of Lautrec's paintings of streetwalkers, pimps, and assorted freaks.

4'11"

QUEEN VICTORIA

1819–1901

"We are rather small for a queen,"
Victoria observed, using the imperial "we."
But homely "Little Vic," the mother of the
British empire, held the throne for sixty-four
years. She was also mother to nine children,
filling the royal houses of Europe with her
many descendants. Considering all the shops
and inns named after her, the family ought
to collect a royalty.

Under 5′

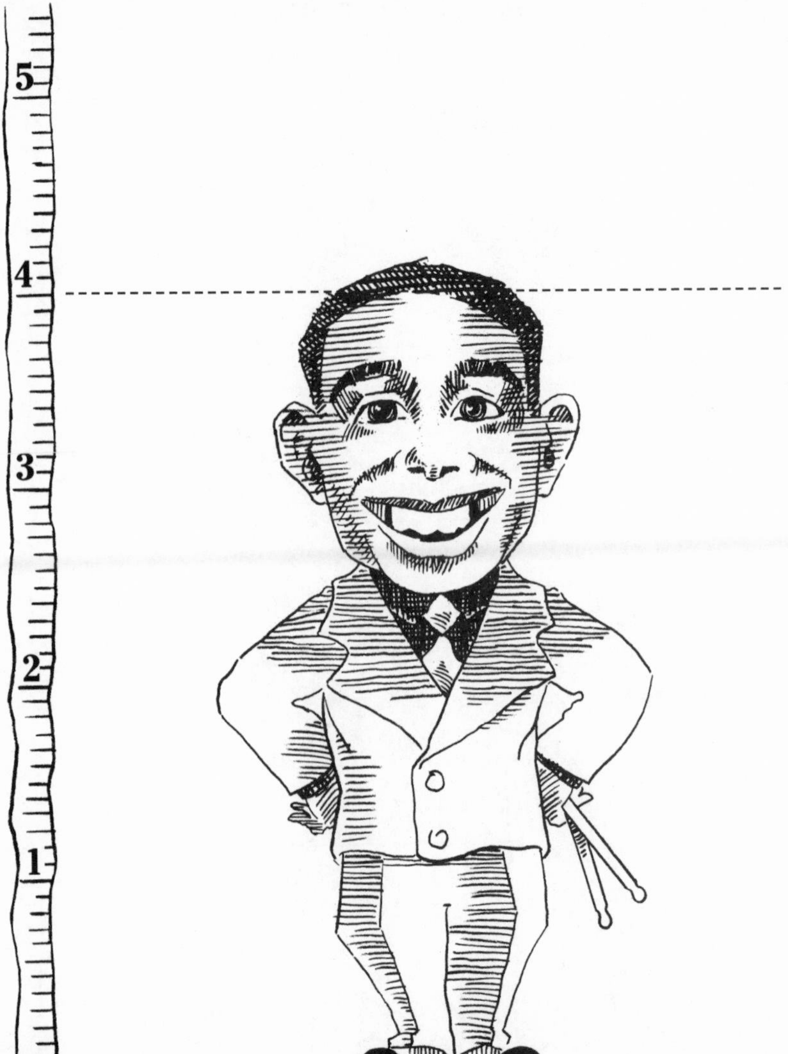
5
4
3
2
1

CHICK WEBB

1909–1939

A hunchbacked dwarf whose toes could hardly reach the bass drum pedal, William "Little Chick" Webb was acclaimed as the first truly great jazz drummer. Leading his band at Harlem's Savoy Ballroom in the 1930s, he piloted Ella Fitzgerald to fame and put audiences so completely under his spell that other musicians called his artistry "spinning the Webb."

Around 4′

DR. RUTH WESTHEIMER

b. 1928

Picture a child half the height of Dr. Ruth,
and you're looking at a brave little girl
who survived the Holocaust. A refugee from
Nazi Germany, this minuscule bundle of
energy, wit, and wisdom turned herself
into today's best-known sex therapist and a
best-selling author.* A typical Dr. Ruth tip:
"If he says 'I don't have any condoms,'
you say, 'Guess what, *I* do!'"

4'7"

*Dr. Ruth Westheimer's *Art of Arousal* (Abbeville Press, 1993) is
available at fine bookstores everywhere.

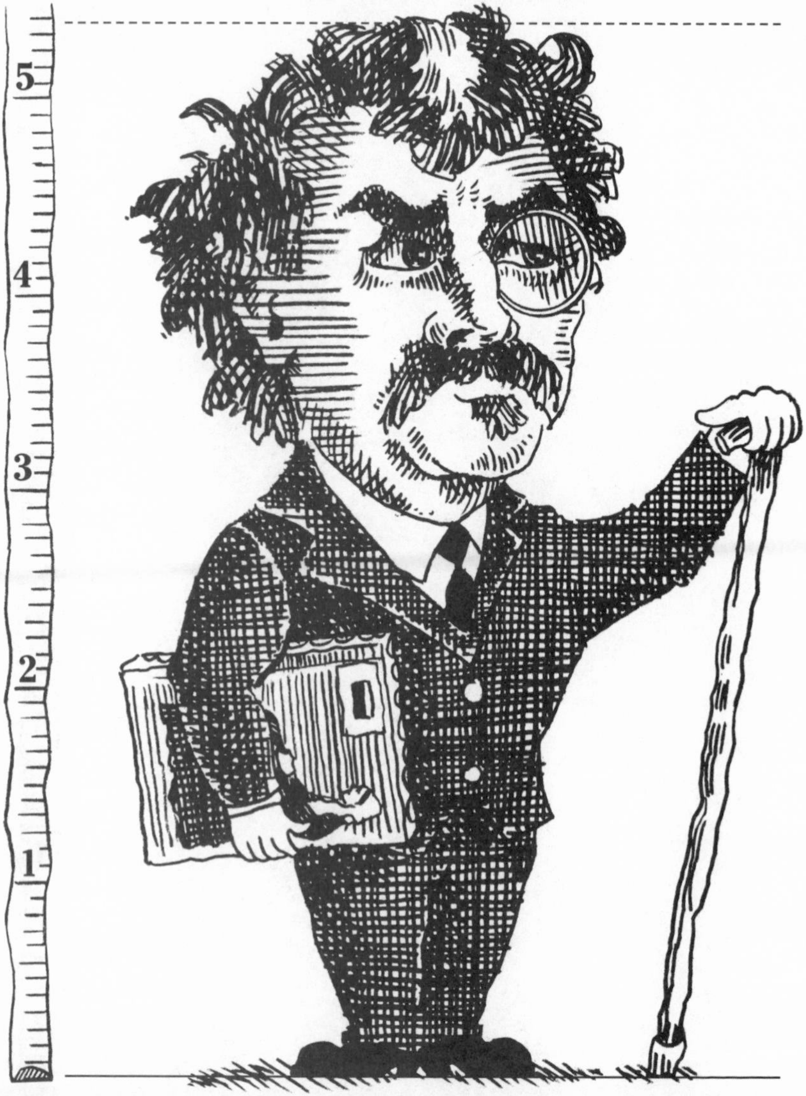
5
4
3
2
1

JAMES ABBOTT MCNEILL WHISTLER

1834–1903

"Jimmy" Whistler titled his most famous painting *Arrangement in Grey and Black* (1872), hardly expecting anyone to care that it was of his mother. Called "a miniature Mephistopheles" by his verbal sparring partner, Oscar Wilde, this devilish dandy of an artist carried a wandlike walking stick once described as being longer than he himself was.

5'4"

WILLIAM WILBERFORCE

1759–1833

Tiny and weak, yet a powerful orator, this
British member of Parliament devoted his life
to ending the slave trade. "I saw what seemed
a mere shrimp," said the Scottish diarist
James Boswell, "but as I listened, he grew . . .
until the shrimp became a whale."
Don't assume this means Boswell shared
Wilberforce's views. He also scolded,
"Begone for shame, thou dwarf with big
resounding name."

5′

Some Borderline Cases

While there are many more "little giants"
than we could fit into this little book, the
celebrities listed here were omitted because
they are or were just a bit too tall
(5'5" or 5'6") to qualify.

Irving Berlin	Jack London
Charlie Chaplin	Zubin Mehta
Winston Churchill	Aristotle Onassis
Sammy Davis, Jr.	Jan Peerce
Fyodor Mikhailovic Dostoevsky	H. Ross Perot
	Marcel Proust
W.E.B. Du Bois	Phil Rizzuto
Albert Einstein	Philip Rose
Roy (Little Jazz) Eldridge	General Philip (Little Phil) Sheridan
Judge Lance Ito	
Alan Ladd	Isaac Stern
Lawrence of Arabia	Jule Styne

Acknowledgments

To write a book about fifty different people one needs the help of even more people. Topping the list is Jane Reed of the University Club Library, the staff at Lincoln Center's Library of the Performing Arts, Ray Wemmlinger of the Hampton-Booth Theatre Library, and numerous helpful souls at New York's Central Research Library, Mid-Manhattan Library, and Brooklyn Public Library.

Additional thanks go to Kathy Shirtleff, Supreme Court Historical Society; Professor Bernard Schwartz, University of Tulsa College of Law; librarian Jacquelyn Brown, Wilberforce University; Brontë Parsonage Museum; National Baseball Hall of Fame; Ed Berger, Rutgers University's Institute of Jazz Studies; Joan Higbee, Library of Congress magic specialist; Benjamin Filene, Houdini Historical Center; and Cindy Huggins, James Anthony, Allan Wilson, and Jane Randall.

For their help and encouragement, I am very grateful to my editor, Meredith Wolf Schizer, agent Carol McCleary, and of course, my family. Last but far from least, I wish to thank Tom Nimen for his brilliant caricatures.

Think small.

Our little car isn't so much of a novelty any more.

A couple of dozen college kids don't try to squeeze inside it.

The guy at the gas station doesn't ask where the gas goes.

Nobody even stares at our shape.

In fact, some people who drive our little flivver don't even think 32 miles to the gallon is going any great guns.

Or using five pints of oil instead of five quarts.

Or never needing anti-freeze.

Or racking up 40,000 miles on a set of tires.

That's because once you get used to some of our economies, you don't even think about them any more.

Except when you squeeze into a small parking spot. Or renew your small insurance. Or pay a small repair bill. Or trade in your old VW for a new one.

Think it over.